the Secret Language
of Flowers

the Secret Language
of Flowers

SAMANTHA GRAY

CICO BOOKS

LONDON NEW YORK

DEDICATED TO MY FATHER, WHO IS ALSO MY BEST FRIEND

Published in 2011 by CICO Books
An imprint of Ryland Peters & Small Ltd

20–21 Jockey's Fields   519 Broadway, 5th Floor
London WC1R 4BW   New York, NY 10012

www.cicobooks.com

10 9 8 7 6 5 4 3 2 1

Editor:
Ingrid Court-Jones

Designer:
Paul Tilby

Illustrator:
Sarah Perkins

A CIP catalog record for this book is available from the
Library of Congress and the British Library.

ISBN: 978 1 907563 87 4

Printed in China

Contents

INTRODUCTION 6

PART 1: COURTSHIP

ANEMONE 10
AZALEA 12
BUTTERCUP 14
CAMELLIA 16
CLOVER 18
GARDENIA 20
GERANIUM 22
GLADOLIUS 24
MISTLETOE 26
PANSY 28
PRIMROSE 30
SNAPDRAGON 32

PART 2: LOVE AND AFFECTION

BLUEBELL 36
CARNATION 38
CHRYSANTHEMUM 44
CROCUS 46
DAHLIA 48
FORGET-ME-NOT 50
HELIOTROPE 52
HONEYSUCKLE 54
LILAC 56
LILY OF THE VALLEY 58
ORANGE BLOSSOM 60
ROSE 62
STEPHANOTIS 66
TULIP 68

PART 3: BEAUTY

AMARYLLIS 74
CHERRY BLOSSOM 76
DAISY 78
IRIS 80
JASMINE 82
LILY 84
ORCHID 88
SNOWDROP 90
VIOLET 92
WATER LILY 96

PART 4: FRIENDSHIP

DANDELION 100
DAFFODIL 102
FOXGLOVE 104
FREESIA 106
HOLLYHOCK 108
HYACINTH 110
LAVENDER 112
MARIGOLD 114
NASTURTIUM 116
PEONY 118
POPPY 120
SUNFLOWER 122
SWEET PEA 124
ZINNIA 126

ACKNOWLEDGMENTS 128

Introduction

Particular meanings—from romantic to religious—have for centuries been attributed to different flowers, yet it was the Victorians who had the idea of sending bouquets, often called "tussie-mussies," to convey secret messages. In a society where strict protocol had to be observed, which in itself tended to contribute to a greater intensity of feeling, an elaborate language based on flower symbolism was developed.

The Victorian language of flowers was mainly one of love and friendship. It might be employed to comment favorably on the personality of the recipient or on shared experiences. Sending bluebells, for example, indicated that the sender considered the recipient loyal and unselfish, while gladioli conveyed sincerity and faithfulness. Some messages were polite and practical—sweet peas indicated "I'm sorry, I must leave."

Flowers were not always tokens of love, however, and more complex and even negative messages could be conveyed. Sending French marigolds, for example, denoted "You are jealous," while orange lilies could mean "You are proud," or even "I hate you."

In a posy each flower had a particular meaning and even the order of the arrangement was significant. Some flowers have multiple meanings, so working out what the giver wanted to say meant considering each in the context of the bouquet. For example, a white lily denoted majesty but also purity and virginity. In this book you will discover the fascinating way in which flowers came by their meanings in folklore and how the Victorians developed these meanings into a sophisticated language.

CHAPTER 1

Courtship

Anemone 10

Azalea 12

Buttercup 14

Camellia 16

Clover 18

Gardenia 20

Geranium 22

Gladiolus 24

Mistletoe 26

Pansy 28

Primrose 30

Snapdragon 32

Anemone

In Greek myth, anemones sprang from the tears of the goddess Aphrodite and the blood of the handsome young god Adonis, as she mourned his death. Aphrodite, who was in love with Adonis, had kept him with her longer than the gods allowed, leading the goddess Persephone to strike him dead in vengeance. In a different myth Chloris, the goddess of flowers, transformed the nymph Anemone, who was loved by both Zephyr, the god of the spring wind, and Borea, the god of the west wind, into a flower. In time, when Zephyr came to claim the nymph, he found her changed into a withered flower—the victim of Chloris's jealousy. Similarly, in Roman mythology, the first anemone was the nymph Anemone, turned into a flower by the goddess Flora, who was jealous that her husband's attention was straying. Having transformed the nymph into a flower, Flora then set the north wind on her—even today, anemones are also called windflowers. These ancient legends are behind the meaning "forsaken," which is sometimes attributed to anemones.

Yet anemones have positive meanings, too. The flowers are thought to bring good luck and protect against evil. People used to gather the earliest flowering anemone they saw, wrap it carefully in a piece of silk, and carry it with them to ward off ill fortune and disease. If you see anemones close their petals, this signals that rain is on the way; and, according to folklore, fairies sleep beneath anemone petals after they close at night. Such associations with predictions and enchantment lead to the meanings of "anticipation" and "expectation."

IF YOU LOVE ANEMONES, you are a gentle, feminine person valued by others for your sweet-natured disposition. You like to bring happiness to those around you, though this can lead you to neglect yourself. Tending to see the good in others, you often fail to see their negative aspects until after you have been hurt. However, you can also see the good in people that no one else sees and therefore encourage their light to shine and grow.

Azalea

zaleas, whose flowers glow jewel-like in a rainbow of hues, were sought in China by Victorian plant collectors and brought to the West. Perhaps due to their desirability during the mid-nineteenth century, azaleas became associated in Europe with the aristocracy. However, their history in China goes back much further—during the Tang Dynasty, azaleas were celebrated by the poet Tu Fu. And today their association with passion, fragility, and femininity means that the name Azalea is becoming increasingly popular for girls in countries such as the United States.

The US cities of Wilmington, North Carolina and Valdosta, Georgia, have the azalea as their symbol, as does São Paulo in Brazil. Azalea festivals are especially popular in parts of the United States and Japan. The flower is also strongly associated with Sagittarius, the ninth sign of the zodiac.

In the West, the meaning of azaleas as a gift has altered subtly over time. Their most dominant meaning today would be "Take care of yourself for me." Azaleas might well be given to a person at risk of neglecting themselves in trying times to express the wish that they don't forget to look after themselves as well as others.

IF YOU LOVE AZALEAS, you probably find that your sensitive and passionate nature leads you to make strong attachments. While this means you are vulnerable to being hurt, it also signifies that you live life to the full. You are the type of person whom people write novels about! With a wild, untamed side to your own nature, you are someone who really enjoys seeing flowers growing in gardens and woodland, rather than cut in a vase.

Buttercup

Buttercups are part of the Ranunculus family. Its flowers range from white to pink, red, yellow, and orange, but it is as golden buttercups that we know them best. *Ranunculus* means "little frog" in Latin. The Roman naturalist, Pliny the Elder, gave this name to the plants because, like frogs, they are often found near water. Other names include greater spearworts, lesser celandines, and coyote's eyes. The latter name derives from a Native American myth in which a bored coyote entertains himself by removing his eyes and tossing them into the heavens, intending to catch them as they fall back to Earth. However, when a buzzard steals them on their way down, the clever coyote fashions new eyes from Ranunculus blossoms.

Buttercups—the small yellow flowers that grow wild—are associated with childhood. Holding buttercups under the chin to see if there is a yellow reflection to indicate if a person likes butter is a well-known children's game. For this reason, buttercups symbolized childishness to the Victorians. The context of the bouquet in which they were sent determined whether the message was one of childlike cheerfulness and innocence, or of immaturity. A posy composed solely of buttercups might be sent as a gentle, affectionate way of reprimanding a loved one for a childish act. A further meaning—wealth—comes from the way in which the golden flowers spread themselves abundantly over meadows. A large bunch of the flowers is a way of saying to someone "I wish you great riches."

IF YOU LOVE THE PINK, RED, ORANGE, OR YELLOW CULTIVATED VARIETIES OF RANUNCULUS, you are someone with captivating individuality. You probably like to wear eye-catching, although not showy, clothes and others admire your unique style. Your wit and clever repartee make you a popular party guest.

IF YOU LOVE BUTTERCUPS THAT GROW WILD IN THE COUNTRYSIDE, you are cheerful, unostentatious, and impulsive. You live life to the full in the present moment and have a sweet and playful temperament. It is probable that your heart belongs in the country, even if you live in a town.

Camellia

In the eyes of the Chinese, the symmetrical petals of the camellia flower reflect the spirit of a lady, and the calyx holding the petals represents the young man who will protect her. The calyx of most plants remains after the petals have dropped, but the camellia's calyx falls with the petals when the flower dies. This symbolizes an everlasting union between lovers. In many parts of China, the camellia is considered the most favorable flower to be worn by young people to attract a marriage partner.

THE BEAUTY OF CAMELLIA FLOWERS INSPIRED VICTORIAN LOVERS TO CHOOSE THEM TO EXPRESS DEVOTION, BUT DIFFERENT FLOWER COLORS VARIED IN MEANING:

THE PINK-FLOWERED CAMELLIA: *"I long for you"*
THE RED-FLOWERED CAMELLIA: *"You are a flame in my heart"*
THE WHITE-FLOWERED CAMELLIA. *"You are adorable"*

Camellias became the height of fashion as a corsage in 1940s America. In Temple City, California, the first Camellia Festival was celebrated in 1945, with people gathering to admire vast floats of flowers. Annual camellia festivals spread across the United States in this decade and in the 1950s.

Unlike some flowers, which can have negative as well as positive meanings, camellias always bring good fortune. Not only are they emblems of love, but they are also lucky, especially when presented to a man.

IF YOU LOVE CAMELLIAS, you have an eternally youthful and hopeful personality. You are a natural perfectionist who enjoys creating beauty and balance in your home. You think carefully before you give away your heart, but once you truly fall in love, it is for ever and you are absolutely loyal to your partner.

Clover

Clover is a Mediterranean plant, which was originally called *clava* by the Romans after the name given to Hercules's legendary three-knobbed club. The Anglo-Saxon term, used in ancient Britain, was *cloefer* or *cloeferwort*. In Ireland, clover is often called shamrock, a name dating back to the ancient Druids who called the plant *seanrog*, which became *shamroag*, then shamrock. They considered the three leaves to be symbolic of the eternals—earth, sea, and sky. In medieval times, its three leaves became the symbol of the Holy Trinity.

Three is Ireland's magic number and so the three-leafed clover or shamrock became a well-known Celtic symbol. Shoots of bright green shamrock appearing on St Patrick's Day are seen to herald the arrival of spring in Ireland, where the plant is strongly associated with love and weddings. It was once believed that no bride should walk down the aisle without clover tucked in both of her shoes, as the plant symbolizes a long and happy marriage and a prosperous life together.

Even more auspicious than the three-leafed clover is its rarer four-leafed cousin. Paintings of Eve in the Garden of Eden sometimes show her carrying a four-leafed clover—the four leaflets signifying faith, hope, love, and luck. According to folklore the four-leafed clover was used as a charm against the devil, witches, snakes, and other dangerous creatures. It was also believed to give its possessors the gift of second sight, so that they could see fairies. While a four-leafed clover is a symbol with positive connotations, clover with more than four leaves is considered an ill omen.

IF YOU LOVE CLOVER, you are someone with a strong sense of the spiritual aspects of nature. You value the past and tradition, and you are drawn to others who are true to themselves just as you are true to yourself. You have a joyous side to your nature and an ability to be completely in the present moment. You particularly dislike artifice and deception in others, and you are adept at discerning it.

Gardenia

**PURITY AND SWEETNESS; SECRET LOVE; JOY;
"YOU ARE LOVELY"**

Favored for their intensely sweet-smelling, creamy-white flowers and evergreen foliage, gardenias were once popular as corsages for women and as buttonhole flowers for men. In France, especially, a gardenia was the traditional buttonhole flower worn by men on important occasions. Today, with their associations of beauty, purity, and love, they are often used in wedding celebrations.

While gardenias are native to China, they were named in 1760 in South Carolina, the United States, to honor the botanist Dr Alexander Garden. More famously, they were associated with the jazz singer, Billie Holiday, who wore gardenias in her hair, calling them her trademark. The gardenia is also the national flower of Pakistan.

In Chinese herbal medicine, gardenias are used to calm anxiety and irritability, and to help treat the menopausal symptoms of insomnia, depression, and headaches. An aromatherapy candle perfumed with gardenia imparts a sweet and soothing scent to the room.

As a gift, gardenias indicate to the recipient how lovely you find him or her, conveying your secret love. For a Victorian lady, accepting a gift of a gardenia flower from a favored suitor would be a cause for great excitement.

IF YOU LOVE GARDENIAS, there is a pure sweetness to your nature like that encapsulated in the flower itself. People crave your companionship because you bring with you a joyfulness that is infectious, benefiting everyone around you. You are an admirer of beauty and have a natural appreciation of symmetry and balance. You have probably made your home a serene and lovely place to return to.

Geranium

Geraniums create a sense of optimism and cheer, whether adding patches of intense color to glorious Mediterranean settings or enlivening gray city streets. In Harper Lee's *To Kill a Mockingbird*, red geraniums outside the neglected house of a character symbolize the good that exists in everyone, even the most corrupt. In the 1950s, after World War Two, red geraniums were often displayed in window boxes, leading people to equate them with a positive new outlook.

The flowers we think of as geraniums are actually pelargoniums. Both true geraniums and pelargoniums belong to the *Geraniaceae* family and are native to South Africa. It was not until the late nineteenth century that experts realized the differences and wanted to call them by separate names, but by this time the name geranium was popular in Europe and America, and plant lovers did not welcome a change. The word geranium is derived from a Greek term meaning "crane," a reference to its long stem. The plant's general message is one of gentility or peace of mind.

To the Victorians, the geranium's varying flowers and leaves suggested a range of subtly different emotions and their leaf shape, color, and scent became as important and evocative as the flowers for conveying a message. While red-flowered geraniums indicated love and desire, those with pink flowers signified grace, gentility, and happiness, and white meant admiration. Silver leaves conveyed a reminder of the past; scarlet-tinged leaves represented an offer of comfort or consolation; and oak-shaped leaves showed true friendship. Even the various scents gave different meanings: rose-scented meant "I prefer you;" lemon indicated an unexpected meeting; and a scent of nutmeg signified "I expect a meeting".

IF YOU LOVE GERANIUMS, you have a resilient and optimistic nature. Your friends value the way you stand by them through thick and thin. You believe in traditional values such as love, loyalty, trust, honesty, and family ties. There is also a romantic, nostalgic side to you, and you are passionate once you have found the right partner.

"Why your hair was amber, I shall divine,
And your mouth of your own geranium's red—
And what would you do with me, in fine,
In the new life come in the old one's stead."

ROBERT BROWNING, "EVELYN HOPE"

Gladiolus

"I AM REALLY SINCERE;" "GIVE ME A BREAK;" LOVE AT
FIRST SIGHT; FAITHFULNESS; STRENGTH OF CHARACTER;
FLOWER OF THE GLADIATORS; SINCERITY

The sword-shaped leaves of the gladiolus give the plant its name—the Latin word *gladius* means "sword." Another name for gladioli is sword lilies. Gladioli are symbolic of integrity and strength of character. *Gladius* is also the Latin root for the word "gladiators," the soldiers who lived or died by the sword.

Once regarded as troublesome weeds in cornfields, gladioli were given the English common name, corn flags. During the nineteenth century many new gladioli were bred around Europe, producing a huge variety of larger, more colorful blooms. In recent years, gaudy gladioli were chosen by the Barry Humphries's television character Dame Edna Everage as her trademark flower, and so became associated with vulgarity. Today, however, gladioli, particularly the more delicate blooms in muted hues, are making a comeback and regaining their popularity. They are easy to grow and make excellent cut flowers.

Gladioli are also associated with romance, and it was once believed that the roots were an aphrodisiac. Receiving a bouquet of gladioli sent the recipient a message that she or he had pierced the giver's heart with passion. Gladioli are the traditional flowers for fortieth wedding anniversaries.

IF YOU LOVE GLADIOLI, particularly those with large, colorful blooms, you have an extrovert personality—perhaps you are even an unashamed exhibitionist. Your wonderful sense of humor constantly wins you invitations to social events. If your favorite gladioli are the more delicate, orchid-like blooms, you also have a need for attention, but mainly from a special person.

Mistletoe

Once thought to have mystical powers, mistletoe became a part of many folklore customs. In Druid wedding ceremonies, the bride and bridegroom kissed under a bunch of mistletoe. It was in eighteenth-century England that the idea of a "kissing ball" of mistletoe at Christmas was introduced, under which a lady could not refuse to be kissed. If she did refuse, she would remain unmarried through the following year. A man should pluck a berry after kissing a woman under mistletoe so that, when the last berry is gone, there is to be no more kissing under that particular bunch.

As a love charm, mistletoe was thought to encourage passion and fertility, while as a magical form of protection against evil it was used to exorcize ghosts—or even to make them speak. A Celtic tradition is to hang sprigs of mistletoe outside homes on New Year's Eve to welcome in the year and to ward off evil, such as witchcraft. Sprigs of mistletoe were also hung over babies' cradles to protect newborns from being taken by the fairies, who would substitute a changeling. Another custom was for farmers to give a bunch of mistletoe to the first cow that calved in the New Year to bring good luck to the whole herd.

A French legend claims that mistletoe was once a tree, but it was cursed after its wood was used to make Christ's cross. Denied the right to grow in the earth, it then had to live parasitically on other plants to survive. In Brittany, France, mistletoe is still called *herbe de la croix*. The English name derived from the belief that the plant sprang from bird droppings. *Mistel* is Anglo-Saxon for "dung" and *tan* is the word for "twig." Mistletoe often grew on twigs covered in bird droppings, and its name means "dung on a twig."

IF YOU LOVE MISTLETOE, you are probably someone who enjoys all the rituals of Christmas and other festive celebrations. You have spiritual, perhaps even clairvoyant, tendencies. With this extra dimension to your personality, other people are drawn to you but some may be envious of you, too.

"The mistletoe hung in the castle hall,
The holly branch shone on the old oak wall."

THOMAS HAYNES BAYLY, "THE MISTLETOE BOUGH"

Pansy

**"YOU OCCUPY MY THOUGHTS;" "THINK OF ME;"
ROMANTIC THOUGHTS; "YOU TICKLE MY FANCY"**

A type of violet, the pansy was a vital ingredient in Celtic love potions. In *A Midsummer Night's Dream*, William Shakespeare echoes this idea when Titania—with pansy juice in her eyes—falls in love with the first creature she sees when she wakes up. The heart-shaped petals were believed to have magical properties—even the power to heal a broken heart.

According to folklore, people should not pick pansies while drops of dew are upon them because this will herald the death of a loved one, and there will be as many tears shed before the next full moon as there were dewdrops. For the Victorians, pansies were traditional St Valentine's Day flowers and they were often exchanged by courting lovers.

In a German legend, pansies once had a strong scent. This was so enticing that people came from far away to smell them, trampling the grass around them so that cattle had nothing to eat. The pansies prayed to God for help and God took away the pansies' scent, giving the flowers great beauty instead.

IF PANSIES ARE YOUR FAVORITE FLOWER, like them, you have great charm. Although you enjoy being noticed, you are never loud or obvious. Your gentle, loving nature attracts many admirers of the opposite sex, but you are also in demand as a kind and loyal friend.

"*And there is pansies, that's for thoughts*"
(WILLIAM SHAKESPEARE, *HAMLET*, OPHELIA IN ACT IV, SCENE V)

Primrose

Primroses are the flowers of first love, making them the ultimate courtship flower. They bloom early in the year—"prim" coming from the Latin *prima*, which means "first." *Prima rosa* means "first rose." While traditional pale yellow, moon-colored primroses symbolize young love or convey meanings such as "I can't live without you," lilac-tinted primroses signify confidence, while red-tinted primroses represent unappreciated merit. The sacred flower of Freya, the Norse goddess of love, the primrose was used in rituals to honor her.

The primrose has always been a favorite subject for poets. Shakespeare refers to the cosmetic properties of primroses in *A Midsummer Night's Dream* and the sixteenth-century English poet, John Donne, chose the primrose as a symbol of womanhood, while some two hundred years later Samuel Taylor Coleridge celebrated the flower itself in his ode "To a Primrose."

Queen Victoria sent a large wreath of primroses to the funeral of the famous British prime minister Benjamin Disraeli, in April 1881, as primroses had been his favorite flowers. When the anniversary of his death approached a year later, a letter to *The Times* suggested that his friends and supporters should wear primrose buttonholes that day.

IF YOU LOVE PRIMROSES, you welcome new enterprises and radiate a fresh energy that brightens the day for everyone around you. You have a tendency to fall in love easily, and perhaps to have crushes on people. Although you may regret an occasional impulsive deed, you generally enjoy the spontaneous way you live your life. You do not let fear stand in the way of pursuing your dreams.

Snapdragon

The botanical name for the snapdragon is *antirrhinum*—*anti* is a prefix meaning "like," while *rhin* means "nose." "Like a nose" provides an appropriate visual image for the shape of the snapdragon's flower. The rounded edges of the flower's upper petals are slightly larger than the lower petals, creating a slight overhang, like the shape of a nose. The English common name, snapdragon, refers to the mouth that you can create by pressing the sides of the bloom and the snapping sound of the petals closing again.

A belief from folklore was that if a suitor hid a snapdragon about his person, he would acquire a devastating allure and an appearance of congeniality. This ancient belief led the Victorians to equate snapdragons with deception during courtship. However, when combined with a purple hyacinth, which expresses an apology, the message could be a plea for the forgiveness of an indiscretion.

Snapdragons are also synonymous with graciousness, kindness, and courteousness. Given by a man to the young lady of his choice, a bunch of snapdragons conveys a compliment about her character. An appreciative guest might also give snapdragons to thank a hostess for her kind hospitality. Used in bridal bouquets, snapdragons are a good luck charm for a fortunate and blessed marriage.

IF YOU LOVE SNAPDRAGONS, this is probably because they were a childhood favorite. Children love to play with the snapping "mouth" of the flowers and snapdragons also bloom in a variety of cheerful colors, increasing their appeal to children. You are likely to be a sweet-natured, playful person who likes to spread happiness wherever you go.

CHAPTER 2

—

Love & Affection

Bluebell 36

Carnation 38

Chrysanthemum 44

Crocus 46

Dahlia 48

Forget-me-not 50

Heliotrope 52

Honeysuckle 54

Lilac 56

Lily of the Valley 58

Orange Blossom 60

Rose 62

Stephanotis 66

Tulip 68

Bluebell

Bluebells are closely linked to the fairy realm: names for them include fairy thimbles, and dead men's bells, because fairies were said to ring the bell-shaped flowers to announce a death in the mortal world. Death was even rumored to be the fairy punishment for any mortal who dared pick or damage the beautiful, delicate flowers. With all the associations with fairies and witches, it was considered unlucky to walk among bluebells at witching hours such as twilight, when the flowers would be full of spells. Perhaps for this reason, too, it is considered unlucky to bring the flower into the house.

The former botanical name for bluebell is *endymion*, which it shares with the mythological Endymion, the lover of the moon goddess, Selene. The goddess put a spell on Endymion, casting him into an eternal sleep so that she alone could enjoy his beauty. Bluebells are also associated with a dreamless sleep, and herbalists used to prescribe a tincture of bluebells to prevent nightmares.

Although it is unlucky to pick bluebells or to bring them indoors, for lovers a walk in a bluebell wood can be full of romantic meaning. It is a way of saying "You have cast a spell on me," "My love is eternal" or, more sadly "I love you, but I cannot be with you."

IF YOU LOVE BLUEBELLS, you are someone who fascinates others, even though you do not try to be noticed. You appear ethereal and a little mysterious, but you are well grounded and practical. Once you make up your mind about someone, you rarely change your opinion, which makes you both a constant friend and an implacable enemy. People who mistake your shyness for timidity are mistaken—there is a strong "true self" beneath your apparent fragility. Once you truly love someone, your love is deep and eternal.

Carnation

The botanical name for the carnation, *Dianthus*, can be translated as divine flower or flower of the gods. The Greek word *dios* means "divine" and *anthos* means "flower." Some scholars believe that the name carnation comes from the word "coronation," because the flowers were used in Greek ceremonial crowns. Others think that the name comes from the Latin *caro*, meaning flesh, referring to the original flower color, or *incarnatio*, meaning incarnation and alluding to the incarnation of God made flesh.

Carnations are one of the world's oldest cultivated flowers, and were first discovered in the Far East. They have a rich historical background of meanings, and are ever popular for their frilly blooms, clove-like scent, and long flowering period. In ancient Greece and Rome, the carnation was a popular motif in the decorative arts. The Romans also referred to the carnation as Jove's flower, because Jove (Jupiter) was one of their most admired gods. In these early times most carnations were shades of pale pink and peach. Through the centuries new varieties have been introduced to include red, yellow, white, magenta, and even striped flowers.

Pinks

Of all the colors, pink carnations carry the greatest spiritual and emotional significance, due to the Christian belief that the first carnations bloomed on the patches of earth where Mary's tears fell as she wept for Jesus carrying the cross. This makes the original pink carnations the ultimate symbol of undying maternal love. In the early part of the twentieth century, carnations became the official flower of Mother's Day. In a Canadian tradition, people used to wear a red carnation on Mothering Sunday if their mother was still alive, and a white carnation if she was not.

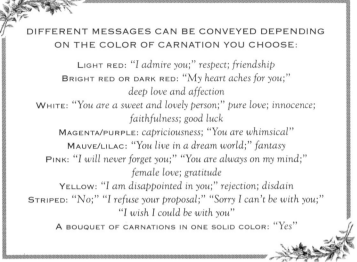

DIFFERENT MESSAGES CAN BE CONVEYED DEPENDING ON THE COLOR OF CARNATION YOU CHOOSE:

LIGHT RED: *"I admire you;"* respect; friendship
BRIGHT RED OR DARK RED: *"My heart aches for you;"*
deep love and affection
WHITE: *"You are a sweet and lovely person;"* pure love; innocence;
faithfulness; good luck
MAGENTA/PURPLE: *capriciousness; "You are whimsical"*
MAUVE/LILAC: *"You live in a dream world;"* fantasy
PINK: *"I will never forget you;"* *"You are always on my mind;"*
female love; gratitude
YELLOW: *"I am disappointed in you;"* rejection; disdain
STRIPED: *"No;"* *"I refuse your proposal;"* *"Sorry I can't be with you;"*
"I wish I could be with you"
A BOUQUET OF CARNATIONS IN ONE SOLID COLOR: *"Yes"*

Dreaming of carnations

The meaning of carnations in dreams is significant, and is even thought to be a way of foretelling future events. If you wake up feeling aware that there were carnations in a dream, this is a portent of extraordinary social success. If you were picking the flowers in your dream, this indicates that you will receive a surprise gift. Dreaming of bright red carnations predicts an exciting love affair in the near future, while white carnations reveal that your status is soon to be pleasingly elevated. A dream of pink carnations heralds domestic happiness. If dark red, or a selection of odd-colored, carnations appear in your dream, you will soon—with the help of good friends—encounter a situation from which you will prosper.

Carnations around the world

In Korea, people wear pink and red carnations on Parents' Day (Koreans celebrate Mother's Day and Father's Day on the same day—May 8) to show love and gratitude toward their parents. Students, children, or young people wear white carnations to honor mothers who are far away or dead. Traditionally in Korea, the superstition that carnations could be used to tell fortunes was widespread. For example, girls would wear a cluster of three carnations in their hair. If the flower at the bottom of the cluster died first, this sadly indicated that the wearer would be miserable for the rest of her life. However, if the top flower died first, her last years would be her worst, but she could hope to have a good life up to then. If the middle flower died first, her earlier years would be a struggle but then life would improve.

Red carnations are very much associated with Slovenia. From the sixteenth century onward, a stylized red carnation became a popular decorative motif, and by the nineteenth century, this motif was used widely in the arts and crafts, such as to decorate furniture or to embroider textiles. It was always worked in red, sometimes combined with a blue design. Representing love, red carnations were combined in a corsage with rosemary and geraniums to signify love, fidelity, and hope. Young women traditionally fastened this corsage to the jackets of young men leaving for recruitment into the Slovenian army.

In Ireland, carnations with a greenish hue are worn on St Patrick's Day. Purple carnations are the traditional funeral flowers in France, given in condolence for the death of a loved one.

IF YOU LOVE CARNATIONS, you have a deep sense of history and tradition, and a strong practical streak. Family ties are important to you, and you express affection warmly to make sure that those close to you feel valued. You tend to have close bonds with a select number of friends rather than spreading your company too thinly. Others appreciate your loyalty, resilience, and loving nature.

Chrysanthemum

In England, chrysanthemums used to be known as corn marigolds. However, once their importation from the Far East began in the sixteenth century, their name gradually changed to that of the Oriental variety, chrysanthemum. The name derives from the Greek words *chrysos*, meaning "gold," and *anthos*, meaning "flower."

Chrysanthemums were considered sacred by the nobility in old China and commoners were not allowed to grow them. The flower was one of the four Chinese "honorable" plants (along with orchid, plum, and bamboo), which are symbols of nobility. To Chinese scholars, the combination of beauty and strength was symbolic of an ideal personality. In China today, chrysanthemum petals are eaten in salads to increase longevity, and chrysanthemum tea is a cure for headaches and depression. According to Chinese feng shui, chrysanthemums bring joy to your home.

Japan acquired chrysanthemums from China at the end of the fourth century CE. To the Japanese, the chrysanthemum was symbolic of the sun and the unfolding of the flower's petals represented perfection. Another belief from Japan is that a chrysanthemum petal placed at the bottom of a glass of wine promotes a long and healthy life.

Years of cultivation have produced chrysanthemum flowers in a huge variety of colors, from white through different shades of red to purple. In Japan there is a "Festival of Happiness" celebrated with chrysanthemums each year. In Europe, chrysanthemums are the flower for thirteenth wedding anniversaries.

In Victorian England, different-colored chrysanthemums conveyed different meanings. Red chrysanthemums meant "I love you," white chrysanthemums signified loyal and honest love, while yellow chrysanthemums sent a message of slighted love.

IF YOU LOVE CHRYSANTHEMUMS, you have strong opinions enlivened by a sunny temperament. You never let the knocks of life get you down for long and your philosophy is always that the glass is half full rather than half empty.

Crocus

Several legends surround the crocus flower. One of the most evocative is that of Crocus, a young shepherd boy who falls in love with Smilax, a beautiful nymph. Impressed by the depth of his devotion, the gods grant him immortality by transforming him into the crocus flower. Then, to allow Crocus and Smilax to be together for ever, they transform her into the evergreen yew tree.

The crocus is dedicated to St Valentine, the Christian martyr after whom St Valentine's Day was named. Valentinus was a Roman physician who dispensed natural remedies, and a Christian priest who prayed for his patients. Practicing Christianity was a crime in the reign of Claudius II, so Valentinus was arrested, imprisoned, and sentenced to death. The jailor's blind daughter was one of his patients and, just before his execution, Valentinus handed the jailor a note for the blind girl in which he had wrapped a saffron crocus, the source of the healing herb, saffron. As the girl opened the note, her sight returned; the first flower she saw was the yellow crocus shining like the sun. The physician had written the message: "From your Valentine" and the day was February 14, 270 CE.

Blue and mauve crocuses are popular, but it is the saffron crocus that has the most meanings attached to it around the world. Saffron was once considered a great dye and was used to color the robes of religious and political leaders. It has spiritual associations for a number of faiths. In Hinduism, for example, saffron is associated with the Supreme Being. Saffron is also known for its culinary uses and for its medicinal properties—in some folk remedies, it was believed to be an aphrodisiac.

IF YOU LOVE CROCUSES, you value relationships with people and put much of your energy into understanding the needs and feelings of friends and family. You have a deeply spiritual aspect to your nature, which you might express in a creative way—such as in writing, painting, dancing, music, or some other activity. You are a healer and you like to take care of others.

LOVE & AFFECTION

Dahlia

EVERLASTING COMMITMENT; CELEBRATION OF LOVE AND MARRIAGE; ELEGANCE; DIGNITY

The dahlia originates from Mexico, where it was discovered by Spanish explorers in the sixteenth century. It is Mexico's national flower, loved for its colorful and long-lasting blooms. The Empress Joséphine imported dahlias to France in the late eighteenth century for the garden she and Napoleon Bonaparte were creating at Malmaison. Joséphine was proud of her dahlia collection and insisted on tending the plants herself—at this time, a dahlia was so valuable that it could be traded for a diamond.

Sometimes referred to as "the queen of the autumn garden," the dahlia blooms from midsummer through to the first frost. Some plants grow very tall and dahlia flowers vary from quite small and delicate to the size of a dinner plate. They grow in a myriad of colors.

Dahlias are rich in meaning. While expressing dignity and elegance, they also symbolize an eternal bond between two people. This duality makes dahlias a perfect bouquet for high-profile weddings—the flowers epitomize graciousness as well as the deep wish that the couple's relationship will remain strong through any trials and tribulations that the future might bring. Dahlias are the fourteenth wedding anniversary flower.

IF YOU LOVE DAHLIAS, you have a natural majesty and an ability to lead others. People turn to you for inspiration and guidance, so you find yourself the central focus of social and work settings. Your grace and charm put everyone at their ease. With your intense loyalty to people and causes, you are always a force to be reckoned with.

Forget-me-not

There are many different legends around how the forget-me-not acquired its name. In one tragic and romantic tale, a young man and woman walking beside the Danube saw some blue flowers on an islet in the river. The man leapt into the river to gather the pretty flowers for his sweetheart, disregarding her protest that the river's current was too strong. He picked the flowers and had almost reached the bank when he was caught in the whirl and surge of the current, and could not hold his course. Looking into the eyes of his beloved, he used the last of his strength to fling the bouquet at her feet and to cry "Forget me not!" before disappearing under the water. His bereaved lover never forgot him and wore forget-me-nots in her hair for the rest of her life.

In Europe, the forget-me-not was considered a wild, rather than a garden, plant up until the latter half of the nineteenth century. According to Anne Pratt in her 1855 work *Flowering Plants of Great Britain*, by the 1850s bunches of forget-me-nots were being sold in Parisian markets "for the purpose of making the gift of love and friendship." Around the same time in Germany, there was a sentimental vogue for planting forget-me-nots around the graves of loved ones.

The botanical name, *Myosotis*, comes from the Greek for "mouse ear," a reference to the shape of the plant's leaves. An old name once used for forget-me-nots was scorpion grass, referring to the curled flower head that was thought to resemble a scorpion's tail. This also led to the superstition that forget-me-nots could cure the scorpion's sting.

IF YOU LOVE FORGET-ME-NOTS, you are a true romantic. As a child you probably loved all the stories of beautiful princesses or damsels in distress being rescued by handsome princes or knights in shining armor. This is what you truly long for—anyone who wants to win your heart needs to sweep you off your feet.

"The blue and bright-eyed floweret of the brook,
Hope's gentle gem — the sweet forget-me-not"

SAMUEL TAYLOR COLERIDGE, "THE KEEPSAKE"

Heliotrope

The Greek word *heliotrope* means "to turn toward the sun"—*helios* is Greek for "sun" and *tropein* means "to turn." The heliotrope features in Greek myths about the sun god, Helios. In one such myth, Clytie, a water nymph, falls deeply in love with Helios, who is enamored of a princess. Clytie sits for nine days and nine nights on the riverbank simply admiring Helios' chariot. As she wastes away to her death with love and longing, Helios takes pity on her and transforms her into a fragrant heliotrope flower. In her new state she is able to keep her vigil for ever. This is how the heliotrope became the symbol for eternal love and devotion. If you look at heliotropes on a sunny day, you will see the plants turn their flowers and leaves toward the sun.

Dreaming of heliotropes signals unrequited love, while heliotrope oils bring about dreams that hold premonitions. Folklore attributes many superstitions to the heliotrope, which is also known as the herb of love. In one example, it was said that if you pick heliotrope blossom in the month of August and use it for good purposes, the good will come back to you. However, if your intentions are unkind, your wickedness will rebound on you tenfold.

The heliotrope was a popular flower in Victorian England, having been introduced from Peru in the mid-eighteenth century via France. The flower's sweet perfume also became popular and, due to the flower's meaning, had intensely romantic associations. In his poem, "White Heliotrope," Arthur Symons (1865–1945) evokes the way in which the scent of the heliotrope worn by a woman will haunt her lover for ever, keeping her eternally in his memory.

IF YOU LOVE HELIOTROPES, you are a deeply romantic person. Heliotropes are a cottage garden favorite, so you have probably seen the large clusters of white, lilac, or blue flowers spilling over fences in country villages. You could never be accused of being fickle—once you give your heart, it is for ever.

Honeysuckle

A climbing plant, honeysuckle is named for the strong, sweet scent of its creamy yellow, pink, or reddish-pink flowers. Once established in a garden, honeysuckle vines are extremely hardy and difficult to kill. Their resilience, combined with their sweet-as-honey fragrance, led to their association with lasting bonds of love and friendship, as well as with sweetness and happiness.

In a Celtic alphabet carved into stones, known as the Ogham alphabet, each letter represented a particular plant or tree. The honeysuckle letter stood for following the path of life like a twisting vine, attracting sunshine and joy.

In Scotland, it was a tradition to use honeysuckle in garlands and decorations for wedding ceremonies to represent the love that holds on through both good and bad times. In French tradition, giving honeysuckle to a partner demonstrates the generosity of your love, while more widely in folklore around Europe, a honeysuckle blossoming near your home foretells a wedding within one year. In China, dreaming of honeysuckle means either that you are feeling passionate about someone or that a would-be lover is fantasizing about you.

IF YOU LOVE HONEYSUCKLE, your natural kindness masks a steely core. Anyone who thinks that, with your amenable disposition, you are going to be a pushover, will soon find themselves mistaken. Like honeysuckle itself, you combine sweetness with resilience—and for this reason, you are likely to form deep and lasting relationships. Your partner and friends know they can rely on you.

"O were my love yon Lilac fair,
Wi' purple blossoms to the Spring,
And I a bird to shelter there,
When wearied on my little wing!
How I wad mourn when it was torn
By Autumn wild and winter rude!
But I wad sing on wanton wing,
When youthfu' May its bloom renew'd."

ROBERT BURNS, "O WERE MY LOVE YON LILAC FAIR"

Lilac

The botanical name for lilac is *Syringa*. According to Greek mythology, Syringa, or Syrinx, was a beautiful nymph who captivated Pan, the god of the forests and fields. Pan chased Syringa through his domain until, finally, Syringa was exhausted and could only escape him by turning herself into a plant. This is the fragrant shrub commonly called lilac.

Lilac is an old French word derived from the Persian word *nilak*, meaning "indigo," which in turn comes from *nila*, a Sanskrit word meaning "light blue." The name Lilac was popular for girls in Europe in the eighteenth and nineteenth centuries.

Lilac's meanings of first love and youthful innocence arise from its flowering time being a harbinger of spring. Purple-flowering lilacs convey the first emotions of love, whereas white- or pink-flowering lilacs are associated with youthful innocence. In Russian folklore, cradling a newborn beneath a lilac bush would bring the child wisdom. In parts of the Mediterranean, including Greece, Cyprus, and the Lebanon, lilac is closely associated with the festival of Easter because it so often blooms around that time. Lilac is also the flower for eighth wedding anniversaries.

There are few flowers as sweetly scented and as beautiful as the lilac, so despite a short flowering season—just a couple of weeks—they are widely grown. The residents of Rochester in New Hampshire call their town "Lilac City" and celebrate an annual two-week-long Lilac Festival. More than half a million people come each year to admire the 1,200 lilac bushes, which include 500 different varieties. In New Hampshire, where lilac is the state flower, residents claim that lilac is "symbolic of that hardy character of the men and women of the Granite state."

IF YOU LOVE LILAC, you have a cheerful and hopeful personality. Even when times are difficult, you believe in a better, sunnier future. This natural optimism creates such a positive energy around you that your hopes and dreams have a habit of coming true.

Lily of the Valley

RETURN OF HAPPINESS; SWEETNESS; MODESTY;
"YOU'VE MADE MY LIFE COMPLETE;" "LET'S MAKE UP"

One of the legends surrounding lily of the valley is that the scented flowers sprang from Eve's tears as she was cast out of the Garden of Eden. Other names for lily of the valley include Our Lady's tears, since the plants were believed to grow from the tears shed by Mary at the Crucifixion. Monks grew lily of the valley for decorating altars and called it ladder to heaven or Jacob's ladder, because the miniature flower bells grow like steps up the stem. The plant has come to symbolize the power that people have to visualize a better world. Blooming in mid May, lily of the valley is also known as the May Lily and is traditionally used for decoration in Whitsuntide festivities and for spring weddings. It is considered the fifth item (after something old, something new, something borrowed, and something blue) that a bride should carry for good luck.

The seventeenth-century English herbalist Nicholas Culpeper claimed that lily of the valley strengthened a weak memory. As a tonic rubbed on the forehead and on the back of the neck, it is said to boost common sense. It is also thought to improve speech. Lily of the valley is still used as a heart tonic, calming and strengthening the heartbeat in the same way as the foxglove but without the risk of poisoning. Men who had been gassed in World War One were regularly prescribed a tincture of lily of the valley as a restorative tonic to reduce blood pressure.

IF YOU LOVE LILY OF THE VALLEY, you are probably known for your sweet-natured disposition. Those who are envious of you may say you are "too good to be true," but they are wrong—you are as kind and generous-spirited as you appear. You like to make everyone happy and, even though you never put yourself in the spotlight, there is something special about you that other people can't help but notice.

"Sweetest of the flowers a-blooming
In the fragrant vernal days
Is the Lily of the Valley
With its soft, retiring ways."

PAUL LAURENCE DUNBAR, "THE LILY OF THE VALLEY"

Orange Blossom

ETERNAL LOVE; MARRIAGE; PURITY; FERTILITY;
PURE LOVELINESS

Using orange blossom as part of the bride's wedding ensemble originated in ancient China, where it was considered an emblem of chastity. Since the orange is unusual in bearing fruit at the same time that it blooms, the blossom also became a symbol of fertility. During the time of the Crusades the custom of incorporating orange blossom into weddings was brought from the East to Spain, from there to France, and then to England in the early nineteenth century.

Queen Victoria was wreathed in orange blossom for her wedding in 1840, setting a fashion for Victorian brides. Some commentators on morality found this trend distasteful due to orange blossom's symbolic link with fertility. Sprigs were braided into wreath-like headpieces for brides to wear over their veils or shaped into tiaras to adorn their hair. Many also carried bouquets of fresh orange blossom. The link between orange blossom and weddings became so ingrained that the phrase "to gather orange blossom" came to mean "to seek a wife." However, real orange blossom was often in short supply because of the cool English climate, so exquisite wax replicas were made into tiaras instead, remaining popular right up until the 1950s.

The fragrant white flowers of Seville oranges are the source of oil of neroli, used in perfumes and flavorings. Neroli was discovered in the seventeenth century and named after Princess Anne Marie of Neroli, in Italy, who used it as her signature perfume. Neroli is both relaxing and a supposed aphrodisiac—offering a practical reason as well as a symbolic one to include orange blossom in wedding bouquets, as it calmed the bride's nerves and encouraged desire before her wedding night. The cosmetic and medicinal properties of oil of neroli have been appreciated in both the East and the West, and it is thought to bring peace and happiness to the mind and body.

IF YOU LOVE ORANGE BLOSSOM, you are a romantic who values long-established traditions. A thoughtful person, you are aware of, and sensitive to, other people's feelings. Your fine eye for detail reveals itself in the clothes you wear, and in your home and work environments.

"A stir of breeze
Touches the fragrant orange blossoms
Glistening with rain,
And the first song of the hototogisu
Floats from clouds that hang upon the hills."

SHUNZEI, JAPANESE COURT POET, "SUMMER"

Rose

LOVE; ROMANCE; BEAUTY; PASSION; COURAGE

"My love is like a red, red rose, that's newly sprung in June..."
ROBERT BURNS

The red rose is the ultimate flower symbol of love and the traditional romantic Valentine's Day gift. For the Victorians, the number of red roses in a bouquet conveyed a particular meaning, and red roses might be combined with roses in other colors to offer further meanings.

Mixing red with yellow roses sends a message of happiness and celebration, while combining red and white roses indicates bonding, harmony, and true love. Whether the flowers are open or are still in bud also conveys meaning. For example, a single, red rosebud symbolizes purity and loveliness, while a bouquet of red roses in full bloom expresses gratitude or congratulations.

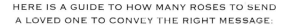

**HERE IS A GUIDE TO HOW MANY ROSES TO SEND
A LOVED ONE TO CONVEY THE RIGHT MESSAGE:**

A SINGLE RED ROSE: *"I still love you;"* *"You are the one;"*
"Love at first sight"
TWO ROSES, ONE RED AND ONE WHITE: mutual love or desire; unity
—often symbolizing commitment, such as a forthcoming marriage
THREE RED ROSES: *"I love you"*
FOUR ROSES: considered unlucky

IN ANY COLOR COMBINATION:
SIX ROSES: *"I want to be yours"*
SEVEN ROSES: *"I am infatuated"*
TEN ROSES: *"You are perfect"*
12 ROSES: *"Be mine"*
50 ROSES: *"My love is unconditional"*

ROSES OF OTHER COLORS

WHITE: *"You're heavenly;"* charm; wisdom; secrecy; sympathy;
humility; youthfulness; and innocence
(a withered white rose means death or loss of innocence)

PALE PINK: *"Please believe me;"* *"You're so lovely;"*
grace; perfect happiness

COMBINING PINK AND WHITE ROSES IN A BOUQUET:
"I love you still and always will"

DEEP PINK: *"Thank you;"* gratitude

ORANGE: *"I want you;"* desire or enthusiasm

PALE CORAL: *"Let's get together;"* sincerity; forming a pact; immortality

YELLOW: *"Welcome back;"* *"Remember me;"* friendship and joy;
sent to a lover can also mean infidelity and jealousy

LILAC: *"I am enchanted by you;"* love at first sight

In Victorian times, the giver chose to leave the thorns on the roses to convey danger or to send a thornless rose to symbolize attachment.

The Romans saw the rose as a symbolic store of secrets. They hung roses above meeting tables and it was understood that anything uttered beneath the hanging roses should never be repeated elsewhere. In Christian lore, a rose bush grew at the site of Christ's death and the red rose is associated with the blood of Christ, its thorns symbolizing his suffering and sacrifice. In the Tarot, the rose represents hope and new beginnings, the loveliness of the flower contrasting with its sharp thorns, which betoken defense against loss, harm, or thoughtlessness.

IF YOU LOVE ROSES, you are the kind of person who brings out the romantic side of your partner. Even though you are a popular person with a busy life and lots of social engagements, you need to be alone to recharge your energies. Secretly, you may be a shy person–but you conceal this by making efforts to put other people at their ease.

Stephanotis

MARITAL LOVE; ETERNAL HAPPINESS; GOOD LUCK

With its creamy white, sweetly scented, star-shaped flowers, stephanotis epitomizes the romantic idea of a beautiful bride in her wedding dress on her big day. In Victorian England, the white flowers also symbolized the bride's chastity before her wedding night. Stephanotis is a perennial favorite for wedding bouquets. The petite delicacy of the flowers also makes them ideal for wearing in a bridal tiara or other small and intricate floral hair ornament.

As a house plant, stephanotis is a popular gift on Mother's Day or Father's Day, or as a way of saying "I love you," "Happy Anniversary," or "Good Luck." It is an appropriate flower to give to someone who is expecting a big life change, as it is believed to bring good fortune.

The word *stephanotis* comes from two Greek words, *stephanos*, meaning "crown," and *otos*, meaning "ear"—the tubular shape of the jasmine-like flowers suggests an ear canal that opens to five crown-like lobes. Stephanotis comes originally from Madagascar and is also known as Madagascar jasmine, waxflower, and floradora, as well as Hawaiian wedding flower, bridal veil, and bridal flower. The sweet scent of the flowers also makes stephanotis a popular perfume ingredient.

IF YOU LOVE STEPHANOTIS, you have romantic ideals and never give up trying to realize these in the real world. Your clarity of vision about what you want means that you tend to succeed in achieving your heart's desire, despite the skepticism of others. You have a sweet and subtle charm that is entirely authentic.

Tulip

Tulips came originally from Persia and Turkey where, a thousand years ago, they grew wild. The Turks of the Ottoman Empire were the first to cultivate tulips and to create hybrid varieties. Poets sang their praises and artists chose their elegant shape to decorate so many beautiful objects that the tulip is considered to be the symbol of the Ottoman Empire.

The name tulip comes from *tulband*, the Persian word for "turban," because the tulip's bulbous shape and rainbow spectrum is reminiscent of the colorful Turkish *tulband*. The word gradually corrupted to *tulipan* and then, much later, became abbreviated to tulip.

TULIPS OF DIFFERENT COLORS MAY BE CHOSEN TO CONVEY EMOTIVE MESSAGES WITH BOUQUETS, OR EVEN THROUGH PLANTING SCHEMES IN GARDENS. FOR EXAMPLE, GIVING SOMEONE A BOUQUET OF RED TULIPS IS A DECLARATION OF LOVE, WHEREAS PLANTING A WHITE TULIP GARDEN, OR BORDER, SYMBOLIZES HEAVEN ON EARTH. HERE IS A GUIDE TO THE MEANINGS OF DIFFERENT-COLORED TULIPS:

RED: declaration of true love; *"Believe me"*
WHITE: heaven; purity; innocence; humility; forgiveness
PURPLE: royalty
VIOLET: modesty
PINK: perfect happiness; best wishes; affection; *"I care about you"*
YELLOW: friendship; *"You have a radiant smile;"*
"There's sunshine in your smile;" cheerful thoughts
ORANGE: desire; passion; enthusiasm; energy
VARIEGATED: *"You have beautiful eyes"*

A Turkish legend may be the source of the meaning conveyed by red tulips. In this legend, Prince Farhad is in love with a girl called Shirin. When Farhad discovers that Shirin has been murdered, he is so overcome with grief that he kills himself by riding his favorite horse over the edge of a cliff. From each drop of his blood on the earth sprang a red tulip.

In ancient Persia, the red tulip was a symbol of passionate love and the king presented a red tulip to his beloved as a symbol of the burning flame of his love. The original red tulips were tinged black at the base of each petal, representing a lover's heart darkened by passion or, as the Persians described it, the king's heart charred to black coal. In nineteenth-century Victorian England, this overt suggestion of sexual attraction did not go down well and the Victorians rarely used tulips to declare their love. Today, however, red tulips are an alternative to red roses for expressing love on Valentine's Day. The tulip is also the eleventh wedding anniversary flower.

Famously, tulips became a national obsession in the Netherlands in the seventeenth century, in the phenomenon dubbed "tulip mania." By 1634 tulip mania really had the population in its grasp, as tulips became the center of speculation, greed, obsession and, ultimately, calamity. At this time tulip prices initially soared and tulips were a symbol of wealth and status, since only the rich could afford them. The craze spread across Europe and wealthy French ladies wore corsages of tulips and dresses made with fabrics that were decorated with tulip designs. In the Netherlands the bulbs became a currency and their value was quoted like stocks and shares—about 10 million bulbs were traded on the stock exchange. In 1637 this speculation became illegal and many people were ruined as the price of tulip bulbs consequently fell. Still, the tulip became the national emblem of the Netherlands during the seventeenth century and it is also the national flower of modern Turkey.

IF YOU LOVE RED TULIPS, you are someone who lives life to the full, almost as if each day could be your last. Your passionate nature does not allow for halfway measures and you throw yourself into relationships or new enterprises completely. **IF YOU LOVE WHITE, PINK, OR LILAC TULIPS,** you have a more serene disposition and enjoy having harmony and balance in your life. You are easily made happy since you have the gift of appreciating the small joys of life. **IF YOU LOVE YELLOW TULIPS,** you have a natural radiance and *joie de vivre* that lights up any room you walk into. **IF YOU LOVE PURPLE TULIPS,** this reveals you as someone who enjoys being a little different and your natural elegance, perhaps even grandeur, ensures that you stand out from the crowd.

CHAPTER 3

—

Beauty

Amaryllis 74

Cherry blossom 76

Daisy 78

Iris 80

Jasmine 82

Lily 84

Orchid 88

Snowdrop 90

Violet 92

Water lily 96

Amaryllis

While amaryllis is known for its showy flowers, the story of Amaryllis in Greek legend is that of a shy and timid shepherdess. She fell deeply in love with Alteo, a shepherd with Hercules's strength and Apollo's beauty. Sadly, her love was unrequited. Amaryllis knew that what Alteo desired most in the world was a flower that outshone any other, and she consulted the oracle at Delphi in the hope that, by attaining such a flower, she might win Alteo's heart. Following the oracle's instructions, Amaryllis dressed in virginal white and appeared at Alteo's door for 30 nights in succession, each time piercing her heart with a golden arrow. When at last Alteo opened his door to her, there before him was a striking crimson flower, which had sprung from the blood of Amaryllis's heart. This legend is behind the meanings of beauty, pride, and determination attributed to amaryllis.

Originally from the Andes mountains of Chile and Peru, the amaryllis was discovered by a plant hunter in 1867. It soon became popular with florists due to its tall stem and large, symmetrical flowers in deep, vibrant shades, some with a star-shaped marking in the center.

The word amaryllis comes from the Greek word *amaryssein* and translates as "to sparkle." Other names sometimes used for amaryllis include belladonna in England, naked lady in the United States, March lily in South Africa, and St Joseph's staff in Portugal. Amaryllis is associated with the astrological sign of Sagittarius, which is characterized by a passion for travel and adventure.

IF YOU LOVE AMARYLLIS, you are likely to be an introvert with an inner extrovert that occasionally finds expression. Alternatively, you might be an extrovert with a secret inward-looking, thoughtful side to your personality. You have a proud, stubborn streak and, once you set your heart on something, you leave no stone unturned to get what you want.

Cherry blossom

It is traditional for people in Japan to gather together to admire cherry trees in flower, a custom known as *hanami*. Anyone planning a *hanami* listens eagerly to the blossom forecast announced by Japan's weather bureau, since cherry trees are only in flower for a couple of weeks. Outdoor parties may then be held in the daytime or at night, when the blossom is bathed in light from paper lanterns. The tradition of *hanami* is said to have begun in the Imperial Court in Kyoto, with blossom-viewing parties enlivened by sake (rice wine) and feasting. Cherry blossom was celebrated in court poetry and was viewed as a metaphor for life itself—beautiful and ephemeral.

For the Japanese, cherry blossom is also associated in legend with the Samurai. When cherry blossom falls, it falls at once. There is a Japanese saying: "A flower is a cherry blossom, a person is a Samurai," meaning that when a Samurai faces death he is unafraid because, like the cherry blossom, he will fall and die at once. In this way the cherry blossom represents not only beauty but also the graceful acceptance that life is temporary. Japan has offered cherry trees to different countries around the world as symbols of peace—for example, in Germany a cherry tree now graces a spot where remains of the Berlin wall lie.

In China the symbolic meanings of cherry blossom are different from those of Japan. For the Chinese, cherry blossom is symbolic of female beauty and dominance—the power that women hold over men through their beauty and sexuality. Within the Chinese herbal tradition, cherry blossom is associated with love and passion.

IF YOU LOVE CHERRY BLOSSOM, you are someone who believes that life is too short to waste, so you live it to the full. You are keen to meet new people and have different experiences. Other people may be amazed at your energy and you do need to take care that you do not suffer from "burn out."

Daisy

The name daisy comes from "day's eye," because the flowers open during the day and close at night. Thought to be more than 4,000 years old, the daisy can be seen as a motif on ancient Egyptian ceramics, and when the Minoan Palace on the Greek island of Crete was excavated, archaeologists found beautiful hairpins finished with gold daisies. In Christianity, the daisy became the plant of St Mary Magdalene and was called the Maudlin daisy.

In a Celtic legend, daisies were the spirits of children who died at birth, sprinkled by God over the Earth to bring cheer and comfort to their bereaved parents. This legend is one of the reasons why daises are associated with innocence.

Children have always loved making daisy chains, and young women tried to find out the fate of a new romance by plucking a daisy's petals while reciting the rhyme "He loves me, he loves me not." In past times, young women used daisies to decorate their hair. In these ways daisies became more associated with innocence and also with youthful beauty. For example, daisies were seen as the perfect posy to give to a young mother of a newborn. Today, they are the traditional fifth wedding anniversary flower.

There is an old English saying that summer has not arrived until you can set your foot upon 12 daisies. Since daisies are still in bloom at the height of summer in temperate countries where thunderstorms are common, they also became known as "thunderflowers" in some regions. A folklore superstition was that dreaming of daises in the spring or summer heralded good luck, but dreaming of daisies in fall or winter foretold hard times ahead.

IF YOU LOVE DAISIES, you have a youthful spirit that will last through your life; even in your older years, you will still be young at heart. Your sunny disposition and sweet nature win you many friends, but you are only truly happy when you are in love.

Iris

A stylized iris is the *fleur de lys* emblem of France and Florence in Italy. It is named after Iris, the Greek goddess of the rainbow, who traveled along the arc of the rainbow to pass messages between the mortal and immortal realms. The name reflects the beauty of the flowers and their myriad colors. Since Iris was a messenger, the flower also indicates a message—often a promise of love—as well as wisdom and valor. Greek men whose mothers or wives had died would often plant an iris on their graves as a tribute to the goddess, Iris, whose duty it was to take the souls of departed women to the Elysian Fields.

The *fleur de lys* shape of the iris flower has always been associated with majestic power. Originally named *fleur de Louis* after King Louise VII of France in 1174, through time the motif became known as *fleur de luce*, meaning flower of light, then *fleur de lys*, which means flower of the lily. It was only during the nineteenth century that the iris ceased to be called a lily. In the twelfth century, King Louis VI became the first French monarch to have the *fleur de lys* emblazoned on his shield. After the English king, Edward III, laid claim to the French crown, the *fleur de lys* was also used on the English coat of arms. By the fourteenth century the *fleur de lys* was often part of the family insignia sewn onto a knight's surcoat.

The iris is also said to be the origin of the scepter, its three petals signifying faith, wisdom, and valor, or, alternatively, perfection, light, and life.

The meaning attributed to irises varies according to their color: purple irises proclaim "You are beautiful," as well as conveying compliments and symbolizing wisdom; blue irises indicate faith and hope; and while yellow irises mean passion, white ones represent purity and perfection.

IF YOU LOVE IRISES, it is because beauty, grace, and elegance are important to you. As a perfectionist, you believe that if a job is worth doing, it is worth doing well. You aspire to achieve great things in your life and to do so with diligence, intelligence, and graciousness.

Jasmine

The name jasmine comes from the Persian word *yasmin*, meaning "fragrant flower;" both are often used as girls' names. Jasmine's scented flowers have a heady perfume, most intoxicating at night, and are said to be an aphrodisiac. The fragrance of jasmine is also thought to be relaxing and antidepressant, making the oil a popular aromatherapy ingredient.

Jasmine originated in the foothills of the Himalayas and the plains of the Ganges. Imported into other countries, it became a favorite of kings and emperors. From the fifteenth century there are records of rulers in Afghanistan, Nepal, and Persia having jasmine planted in their gardens. In China, in the Sung Dynasty, the Emperor is recorded as having hundreds of pots of jasmine moved around the palace so he could enjoy the fragrance.

In ancient Asia, the scent of jasmine was believed to penetrate the deepest parts of the soul, opening up emotions. In India, jasmine is said to evoke a lover—but it is also given as a religious offering symbolizing divine hope. Jasmine garlands have long been popular for Indian weddings.

Wearing the small, star-shaped flowers in the hair is an Eastern tradition. They represent an appreciation of motherhood in Thailand, while in China they are considered the ideal emblem for feminine kindness. In Eastern cultures, burning jasmine oil attracts love, wealth, and prophetic dreams. Jasmine is said to indicate grace and delicacy, sensuality and cheerfulness.

The message conveyed by giving jasmine varies depending on the type and color: white jasmine means amiability; yellow signifies grace and elegance; Spanish jasmine denotes sensuality; and Indian jasmine means attachment.

IF YOU LOVE JASMINE, you believe that beauty is both spiritual and physical—and you take care to relax and recharge your mind and body. Aware that many people spend a lot of time "doing" and not much time "being," you have a strong sense of self and tune in to your intuition. This gives you a quality of stillness that others find deeply attractive.

Lily

FEMALE BEAUTY AND SEXUAL ATTRACTIVENESS; PURITY;
FERTILITY; MAJESTY; WEALTH; CHARM AGAINST EVIL;
DEATH OF A LOVED ONE

The lily was first discovered growing in the garden of an ancient villa in Amnisos, Crete, about 1580 BC. The villa had been built in the Minoan period, when the lily was a sacred flower dedicated to the Minoan Goddess Britomartis, or Dictynna. After the decline of the Minoan civilization, the white lily was dedicated to the Greek goddess, Hera, the wife of Zeus. According to legend, Zeus fathered Hercules with Alceme, a mortal woman. Desiring his son to be nursed by a goddess, he drugged Hera and brought the baby Hercules to her, placing him at her breast. When Hera awoke, she flung the baby away from her in horrified surprise. Some of her milk gushed through the heavens, creating a cluster of stars—the Milky Way—and some drops fell to the Earth, from which grew the first white lilies.

The Madonna lily

In Christian mythology, lilies sprang from the tears of repentance shed by Eve as she learned she was pregnant after her expulsion from the Garden of Eden. The white lily was also designated the special flower of the Virgin Mary, thus becoming known as the Madonna lily. One legend tells how the flower was yellow until the moment that Mary picked it. Another describes how, when Mary's tomb was opened to show Thomas that her body had been assumed into heaven, the place was filled with lilies. The lily became the symbol of the Annunciation, the white petals representing Mary's body and the golden anthers her soul rising to heaven. In medieval paintings, saints are shown bringing white lilies to Mary and the baby Jesus. Another Christian tale featuring the lily is that of St Catherine who converted her pagan father to Christianity when the previously scentless Madonna lily produced its exquisite perfume. In this way, lilies became synonymous with beauty, hope, and life.

"The modest rose puts forth a thorn,
The humble sheep a threat'ning horn:
While the Lily white shall in love delight,
Nor a thorn nor a threat stain her beauty bright."

WILLIAM BLAKE, "LILY"

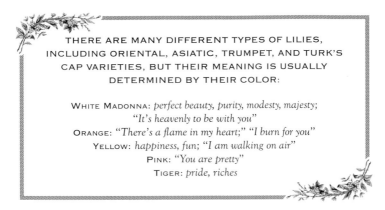

THERE ARE MANY DIFFERENT TYPES OF LILIES,
INCLUDING ORIENTAL, ASIATIC, TRUMPET, AND TURK'S
CAP VARIETIES, BUT THEIR MEANING IS USUALLY
DETERMINED BY THEIR COLOR:

WHITE MADONNA: *perfect beauty, purity, modesty, majesty;*
"It's heavenly to be with you"
ORANGE: *"There's a flame in my heart;" "I burn for you"*
YELLOW: *happiness, fun; "I am walking on air"*
PINK: *"You are pretty"*
TIGER: *pride, riches*

In both the pagan and Christian traditions, the lily is a symbol of chastity until marriage and of fertility thereafter—today, lilies are the thirtieth wedding anniversary flower. In ancient Egypt, the lily's most salient meaning was that of fertility. In ancient Greek and Roman marriage ceremonies, brides sometimes wore a garland of lilies for purity, mixed with ears of wheat, symbolizing abundance. Later, European folk tales described a tradition of approaching an expectant mother holding a lily and a rose— the lily symbolized a boy and the rose a girl. This allowed the mother-to-be to choose which gender she would prefer her child to be.

In medieval times, lilies symbolized female beauty, sexuality, and destiny. To dream of lilies in spring foretold a happy, prosperous marriage, but to dream of them in winter signified frustration of hopes or, worse, the death of a loved one. From folklore there were tales of lilies appearing mysteriously around the graves of people executed for crimes they did not commit. There was also a belief that planting lilies in a garden protected it from ghosts and evil spirits. Lilies have long been associated with death and used as a funeral flower, because they symbolize that the soul of the departed has been restored to innocence.

IF YOU LOVE LILIES, you are a deeply feminine person who is able to tap in to your intuition about people and situations. Others can see you as something of a *femme fatale* because your charisma seems irresistible. In fact, you are much more pleasant than the label *femme fatale* implies, and you make a strong and loyal friend.

Orchid

The name orchid comes from the Greek *orchis*, meaning "testicle," because of the shape of the bulbous tubers. The original ancient Greek association with virility and manliness derived from the ability of the orchid to grow anywhere and to bloom resiliently under any conditions—a characteristic that also gives orchids the meaning of strong love and attachment. In folklore the tubers were associated with fertility. A Greek old wives' tale advised that women could choose the sex of their child by means of orchid tubers. If the father ate large tubers, the child would be male; if he ate small tubers, the child would be female. In ancient China the orchid flower was given as a sign that the recipient would have many children. Men might display orchids or give them to women in a flirtatious way, which conveyed their sexual interest.

In Victorian England, the orchid flower became symbolic of a lady whose beauty was rare and delicate. This was a shift of meaning away from the orchid's association with virility and manliness. The rarity of some orchids and the rise in the popularity of orchid collections in Victorian England also meant that the flower became associated with luxury. To the Victorians, this meant that to give such a flower was an expression of deep emotion.

There are many different types of orchids blooming in curious shapes that have led to a variety of intriguing common names, such as ladies' tresses, adder's tongue, dead men's fingers, and ram's horns. All orchids have spot-like markings. Christian legend relates that orchids were growing at the foot of the Cross and that Christ's blood dropped onto the flowers, causing them to bear the stains ever since.

IF YOU LOVE ORCHIDS, you undoubtedly have a taste for luxury, style, and elegance. This does not mean that you are a superficial person—far from it. You are likely to be thoughtful, well read, and a witty conversationalist.

Snowdrop

BEAUTY OF SPIRIT; HOPEFULNESS; NEW BEGINNINGS; CONSOLATION

As an emblem of early spring, snowdrops have a natural association with hopefulness and the emergence of beauty and joy. Yet this association has another source, too. In Christian mythology, Eve sat weeping after her expulsion from Eden. Since the Fall, no flowers had bloomed and snow fell constantly. An angel came to talk to Eve and comfort her. Catching a snowflake in his hand, he breathed on it and let it fall to the ground, where it became the first snowdrop. In this way, the snowdrop came to signify new and beautiful beginnings, as well as consolation.

From German folklore, a different snowdrop myth tells the tale of how God created all the things on Earth, but the snow was sad to find itself icily transparent and invisible. God told the snow to ask the flowers if they would give it some of their color. The snow asked each flower in turn and every one of them refused, leaving the snow sadder than ever. Finally, the snow asked a little white flower, which agreed sweetly to let the snow have some of its pure whiteness. In perpetual gratitude, the snow allows its friend the snowdrop to be the first of the flowers to bloom each year.

Snowdrops come originally from Switzerland, Austria, and other parts of Europe. Its botanical name, *Galanthus nivalis*, means "milk-white flower." Despite the snowdrop's meaning of hopefulness, the Victorians also associated the flower with death, since its bell-shaped head hovers just over the ground where the dead are buried. For this reason, it was considered unlucky to pick snowdrops and take them into one's home.

If you love snowdrops, you are a generous-spirited person who likes to bring hope and gladness to everyone around you. Despite your quiet demeanor, you have great courage and you are often the first to try something new. Yours is a sensitive soul, so you need to take care that your giving nature does not get exploited.

"Many, many welcomes,
February fair-maid!
Ever as of old time,
Solitary firstling,
Coming in the cold time,
Prophet of the gay time,
Prophet of the May time,
Prophet of the roses,
Many, many welcomes,
February fair-maid!"

ALFRED, LORD TENNYSON, "THE SNOWDROP"

Violet

A variety of extraordinary legends surround the violet. In one ancient Greek myth, the amorous god Zeus, who was in love with Lo, a lovely nymph, sought to hide her from his wife Hera. He turned Lo into a white cow so as not to arouse Hera's suspicion. However, when Lo wept over the taste of the coarse grass she was obliged to feed upon, Zeus transformed her tears into sweet-smelling violets that only Lo was allowed to eat.

In another Greek legend, Ion, the founder of Athens, was welcomed by water nymphs, who gave him violets as a token of their good wishes. The violet became the emblem of Athens, symbolizing the water nymphs' beauty, innocence, and modesty, and a favorite flower to display in homes, at weddings, and on religious shrines. Like the ancient Persians, the Greeks believed that an infusion of violets helped to ease a broken heart—even today, violets may also be known as heartsease.

In a Roman myth, Venus, the goddess of love, argued with Cupid about who was more beautiful—herself or a group of young girls. By declaring that the girls were more attractive, Cupid sent Venus into such a rage that she beat her rivals until they were blue with bruising and turned into violets. The Romans decorated their banqueting tables with violets in the belief that they would provide a charm against drunkenness, while wearing a coronet of violets the next day would help to relieve a hangover. To the Romans, violets also had associations of sweet innocence and they often placed the flowers on the graves of small children.

Modesty

Another folklore name for violets was flower of modesty, because their flowers hide in their leaves, and Our Lady's modesty, since they were supposed to have blossomed for the first time when Mary said, "Behold I am the handmaid of the Lord," in response to the Angel Gabriel telling her she was to bear the son of God.

"Down in a green and shady bed,
A modest violet grew;
Its stalk was bent, it hung its head,
as if to hide from view"

JANE TAYLOR, "THE VIOLET"

A medieval Christian legend describes how violets once had sturdy, upright stems until the day that the shadow of the Cross fell upon them. Forever after, the flowers bowed their heads in shame at what humanity had done. Violets were often used in Good Friday ceremonies for this reason.

An English myth tells the story of King Frost, who felt lonely in his harsh and solitary ice palace. Eventually, he decided to look for a pretty girl to make him happy. His courtiers found a shy girl called Violet and, falling under her spell, he relented and promised his people six months of milder weather. Violet pleaded with the king to allow her to see her people again and, since he loved her, he granted her wish to visit them each spring. His only condition was that she appear in the mortal realm in the form of a plant, coming back to her husband's icy home each winter.

Napoleon and Joséphine

In France, violets became strongly associated with Napoleon Bonaparte and the Empress Joséphine. She wore violets on their wedding day and on each anniversary Napoleon sent her a posy of violets. Joséphine grew an assortment of violets in her garden, setting a trend in France. At her funeral, violets were showered down upon her coffin as it was lowered into the ground. After he had been exiled to St Helena, Napoleon asked to visit Joséphine's tomb in 1814. He picked some of the violets growing around her grave and they were found in a locket around his neck when he died. Napoleon was nicknamed Corporal Violet or Le Père Violet.

Later, Napoleon III chose the violet as his personal symbol. When he first met with his future wife, Eugénie, she was wearing a violet gown and her hair was decorated with fresh violets. She held a posy of violets at their wedding and the flowers became the couple's special anniversary symbol.

The deep purple *Viola odorata* produces sweet-smelling oil that is used in perfumes. Violet is the flower of February.

Although all violets symbolize beauty, purity, and are a charm against evil, different colors have specific meanings. Blue violets indicate faithfulness, proclaiming "I will always be true;" white denote modesty and the desire to take a chance; and yellow violets signify "You are worthy of happiness."

IF YOU LOVE VIOLETS, you are someone who attracts a lot of attention, even though you never push yourself forward. This has much to do with your charm and sweet nature. Yours is a beautiful soul and this is probably reflected in your outward appearance.

Water lily

Found in shallow ponds, streams, and lakes, the water lily grows in fresh, still water where there is no current. Its botanical name is *Nymphaea*, from the Greek word for "nymph." In Greek mythology water nymphs were beautiful, supernatural women who haunted the places where water lilies grow, and it is from this association that the water lily means feminine beauty. The flower has fascinated artists through the ages, most famously the Impressionist painter, Claude Monet (1840–1926).

In a South American Indian legend, the water lily was once a star that fell from the sky and changed into a flower. Another legend from the Amazon relates the tale of a girl whose tribe believed that a powerful warrior king lived in the moon. She fell so in love with the moon king that she refused to marry any boy from her tribe. Instead, she would stare into the sky at night, trying to see the face of her beloved. One night, when the moon was full in a cloudless sky, the girl ran through the jungle, desperate to meet her warrior. She came to a glass-like lake in which an image of the moon was reflected and she plunged in to be with her beloved. The warrior in the moon watched helplessly from above as she drowned. He did not have the power to bring her back to life, but was so moved that he made her into a star on Earth—the water lily. The Amazon water lily is a giant, beautiful flower whose large leaves are firm enough to bear the weight of a child. The flower only opens completely on clear and cloudless nights when the moon is full.

The water lily is an important flower in Buddhism, as it is associated with enlightenment. Each flower color has a different meaning: white water lilies signify mental purity and spiritual beauty; crimson denote love and passion; blue water lilies represent knowledge; and purple flowers, mystic powers.

IF YOU LOVE WATER LILIES, you are a pure spirit. You believe in the fundamental goodness of human nature and the universe, even though you are not blind to what happens in the world. A non-judgmental person, you give acceptance and love to others, who bask in the serenity that surrounds you. When you fall in love, you are unshakeable in your loyalty.

CHAPTER 4

—

Friendship

Dandelion 100

Daffodil 102

Foxglove 104

Freesia 106

Hollyhock 108

Hyacinth 110

Lavender 112

Marigold 114

Nasturtium 116

Peony 118

Poppy 120

Sunflower 122

Sweet pea 124

Zinnia 126

Daffodil

"I wander'd lonely as a cloud
That floats on high o'er vales and hills,
When all at once I saw a crowd,
A host of golden daffodils."

WILLIAM WORDSWORTH, "I WANDERED LONELY AS A CLOUD"

Reliable in returning every spring, daffodils are a reminder that beauty can survive even the harshest winter. For this reason, they have come to symbolize goodness prevailing through severe tribulations. Give a bunch of daffodils to someone as a token of forgiveness or to show that you appreciate their honesty. A single daffodil is considered unlucky, however, signaling unrequited love or foretelling a misfortune. In medieval Europe, it was believed that a drooping, single daffodil was an omen of death.

Positive superstitions also surround this flower. While the Romans believed its sap could heal wounds, in Arabia the flowers were thought to be an aphrodisiac. According to Chinese feng shui, daffodils forced to bloom in the New Year bring luck for the next 12 months. Closely associated with the festival of Easter, the daffodil is the national flower of Wales because it blooms on March 1, the feast day of St David, the patron saint of Wales. In the UK, Prince Charles is paid one daffodil annually for uncultivated land in the Isles of Scilly.

IF YOU LOVE DAFFODILS, you are a loyal friend and lover who takes pleasure in bringing happiness to those around you. You are a giving person with a tendency to conceal any sadness you might feel beneath a sunny smile that brightens the day of everyone you meet. You are a truthful person and a hopeless liar. Your warm personality and ability to remain strong in difficult situations win popularity and admiration.

"Welcome children of the Spring,
In your garbs of green and gold,
Lifting up your sun-crowned head
On the verdant plain and wold."

FRANCES ELLEN WATKINS, "DANDELIONS"

Dandelion

The name dandelion comes originally from the French, *dents de lion*, because the pointed leaves look like lions' teeth. From Roman times, and probably before, dandelions have been used for culinary and medicinal purpose. The young leaves are an edible salad crop, dandelion root is a coffee substitute, and the flowers can be used to make wine.

The dandelion is well known for its bright yellow flowers, which leave behind a puffball of downy seeds for the wind to scatter. It is the only flower that represents three celestial bodies: the sun (the flower), the moon (the puffball seedhead), and the stars (the seeds blown into the air.)

Like daisy flowers, those of the dandelion open to greet the morning and close in the evening as darkness falls. Dandelions have the longest flowering season of any plant and, according to folklore, coming into flower is a sign that the honey bee season is starting. Children love to blow the puffball seeds, making a wish as they do so. Dandelion seeds can travel up to 5 miles (8 km) away from their source.

Although traditionally the dandelion was associated with loyalty, faithfulness, and happiness, the flower was assigned a new meaning in Victorian England. At this time, the dandelion's sun-like flower was seen as symbolizing coquetry rather than cheerfulness. To dream of dandelions was unfortunate, since this indicated that a loved one was being deceitful.

IF YOU LOVE DANDELIONS, you are someone who likes to have fun and doesn't take life too seriously. You enjoy being the center of attention and like to be out and about doing things. Family and friends are important to you, and you are good at remembering special anniversaries and organizing social reunions. Other people bask in the warmth of your sunny personality.

Foxglove

A woodland plant that has an historic association with magic and mystery, the foxglove has acquired an assortment of descriptive popular names in the past, including folksglove, fairy cap, fairy petticoat, fairy thimble, and witch's thimble. Foxgloves can convey either positive or negative meanings and, for the Victorians, the clue lay in the other flowers in the bouquet. For example, if given with purple hyacinths, the message could be "I am sorry I deceived you," but with, say, bluebells, it could be "I will always be fascinated by you."

A myth from English folklore explains how foxgloves acquired the common name folksgloves—the folk were the fairy folk and the gloves were the foxglove blossoms that the fairies put on foxes' toes, so that they could steal silently up to chicken coops. Children were told that picking foxgloves offended the fairies—a belief that also served to keep them from ingesting this poisonous plant. The names dead men's bells and witches gloves also derive from the presence of powerful chemicals in the plants that can heal in small amounts and kill in large ones.

Many myths from different parts of the world surround foxes and foxgloves. Foxes were supposed to have supernatural powers of deception and this contributed to the flower developing the meaning of insincerity. For example, in Chinese and Japanese folklore, foxes had the ability to transform themselves into humans. Also, people killed them for their bushy tails, which were thought to act as a charm against evil. According to one legend, the foxes begged God for protection, so He put foxgloves in fields and woodlands so that the bell-shaped flowers could ring a warning to the foxes as hunters approached.

IF YOU LOVE FOXGLOVES, you have a wild and untamed nature–no matter how demure you might appear to be on the surface. With your individual spirit, you do not like to be told what to do by others. People find you intriguing, but sometimes you wish they'd keep their curiosity to themselves. You are generous with the energy you give to friends, but you need time alone to recharge.

FRIENDSHIP

Freesia

reesias were first discovered in South Africa two hundred years ago and were almost unknown in the West until the 1950s. These graceful flowers are popular for weddings, as they combine beauty and fragrance, as well as conveying trust and faithfulness. Such associations contribute to freesias being the seventh wedding anniversary flower. Their elegant appearance has meant that, recently, they have been deemed an ideal gift for people who have performed graciously under pressure. Well-loved as cut flowers, freesias are also grown for their scent, which is used in perfumes, bath oils, and soaps.

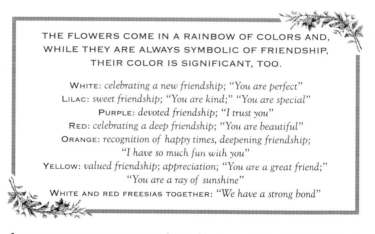

THE FLOWERS COME IN A RAINBOW OF COLORS AND,
WHILE THEY ARE ALWAYS SYMBOLIC OF FRIENDSHIP,
THEIR COLOR IS SIGNIFICANT, TOO.

WHITE: *celebrating a new friendship*; *"You are perfect"*
LILAC: *sweet friendship*; *"You are kind;"* *"You are special"*
PURPLE: *devoted friendship*; *"I trust you"*
RED: *celebrating a deep friendship*; *"You are beautiful"*
ORANGE: *recognition of happy times, deepening friendship*;
"I have so much fun with you"
YELLOW: *valued friendship; appreciation*; *"You are a great friend;"*
"You are a ray of sunshine"
WHITE AND RED FREESIAS TOGETHER: *"We have a strong bond"*

IF YOU LOVE FREESIAS, you are someone who sees friends as an "alternative family." You do much to ensure that your friends feel special and valued. Being a kind person whom friends can trust sometimes means that you receive back all the positive energy you give out; at other times, it leaves you feeling disappointed that others are not as giving. Ultimately, though, your sweet and trusting nature wins through and earns you the happiness you deserve.

Hollyhock

An English cottage garden favorite, hollyhocks originated in the Middle and Far East. Tall and showy, they call more attention to themselves than any other flower in the border—leading to their meaning of ambition. White hollyhocks, in particular, are associated with female ambition. This is because the Victorians considered white to be the most bohemian and unconventional of flower colors. Hollyhocks are also the thirteenth wedding anniversary flower.

Treasured in ancient Egypt for their beauty and medicinal value, hollyhocks were even woven into funeral wreaths for the pharaohs. During harvest celebrations, the ancient Greeks offered hollyhocks to Apollo, the sun god, so that he would continue to allow the sun to shine and produce abundant crops. From this tradition comes the hollyhock's association with fruitfulness and fertility.

The ancient Greeks used hollyhock roots to treat all kinds of ailments from indigestion to earache and toothache, and they are also used in Chinese medicine. The flowers were popular in the gardens of ancient Rome, where they were usually planted alongside roses and lilies. They are also known by their Latin name, *Alcea rosea*.

Given to a friend, hollyhocks convey emotional support and attachment—the tall flowers grow supported by walls and fences, signifying the growth of a successful relationship in which each person is able to develop their full potential with the support of the other.

IF YOU LOVE HOLLYHOCKS it is because, like the flowers themselves, you love to stand out from the crowd. While you cannot help showing off your achievements, you are a loyal and caring person—always there to support friends in need. You are someone people turn to for comfort and reassurance, because there is a maternal side to your gregarious nature.

Hyacinth

The beauty and fragrance of hyacinth flowers is celebrated each year on March 7 on World Hyacinth Day, when the plants are in full bloom in northern hemisphere countries. Victorian ladies used hyacinths on their own in a bouquet to convey a simple feeling, or with other flowers to send more complex messages.

Hyacinths owe their name and meaning to Greek mythology. Hyakinthos was a handsome young Greek adored by the sun god, Apollo. But Zephyr, the god of the west wind, was also fond of Hyakinthos and became jealous of their friendship. One day, when Apollo was teaching Hyakinthos to throw the discus, Zephyr blew the discus at Hyakinthos, killing him. The hyacinth flower sprang from his blood and Apollo transmuted Hyakinthos's body into a constellation in the heavens. While hyacinths bloom in a variety of colors, it is the purple hyacinth that most takes its meaning from this myth, since it represents a request for forgiveness.

THE DIFFERENT HYACINTH FLOWER COLORS CONVEY THE FOLLOWING MEANINGS:

PURPLE: sorrow, "I am sorry;" "Please forgive me"
BLUE: constancy, sincerity
RED OR PINK: Playfulness, sportiness
WHITE: loveliness, "I'll pray for you"

IF YOU LOVE HYACINTHS, you are a trustworthy friend who is sporty and fun to be with. A good communicator, you articulate your thoughts and feelings clearly. However, your impetuosity can mean you act rashly and find yourself having to apologize for your actions. You are easily forgiven, because people value your sincerity and your ability to make things happen.

Lavender

Lavender's botanical name, *Lavandula*, may derive from the Latin *lavare*, meaning "to wash," or from *livens* or *lividus*, meaning "bluish." People have valued this aromatic herb for centuries. It was popular in ancient Greece and Rome, where its spiritual and medicinal therapeutic qualities were appreciated. Lavender not only has a relaxing influence, but it is also a natural antiseptic. The Romans were responsible for spreading the use of lavender throughout Europe, taking it wherever they went for use in their bathing rituals.

In Christian legend, lavender received its lovely scent after Mary placed Jesus' swaddling clothes on a bush to dry. Mary's clothes turned blue after touching the lavender flowers. From this holy association, lavender became symbolic of cleanliness and purity, as well as gaining a reputation as a lucky charm against evil. Drying garments and linen by draping them over lavender bushes was once a popular practice—one that still has its merits.

The soothing effects of lavender have led to its association with compassion and healing. The English herbalist Thomas Culpeper (1514–1541) recommended it not only for various physical complaints, but also for emotional ones, such as "tremblings and passions of the heart." During both World Wars, lavender was commonly used as an antiseptic to help heal wounds and burns.

A tradition from folklore was to give women in labor a bunch of lavender to hold, since squeezing the fragrant sprigs would give them the courage they needed for childbirth. Another folklore belief was that holding a bunch of lavender or inhaling its scent would enable people to see ghosts.

IF YOU LOVE LAVENDER, you are a warm-hearted and nurturing person who loves to look after others—and probably animals and plants, too. You have a serene presence founded on a strong sense of self and deeply held moral values of kindness and compassion.

"Here's your sweet lavender
Sixteen sprigs a penny
That you'll find my ladies
Will smell as sweet as any."
LAVENDER SELLERS' CRY, LONDON, C.1900

Marigold

An association with the astrological sign of Leo, the lion—an animal renowned for its brave heart—gives the marigold its meanings of courage, creativity, and passion. According to Christian legend, the marigold was once known as Mary's gold. During the Flight into Egypt, the Holy Family was accosted by thieves but, when they opened Mary's purse, only marigolds fell out. For this reason the early Christians scattered marigold flowers around statues of Mary, the blossoms representing coins.

A belief from Welsh folklore was that a storm was on its way if marigolds did not open early in the morning. The botanical name, *Calendula*, derives from "calendar," because the marigold has always been associated with the sun's journey across the sky. The Victorians believed that you could set your watch by the hour the marigold opened and closed its colorful petals.

A less positive association comes from West Country folklore in England, where picking or staring at the flowers for too long was believed to turn people into alcoholics.

Marigolds are also symbolic of psychic power. They were once stuffed into, or under, pillows by those seeking prophetic visions—particularly by girls seeking to dream of their future husbands. A marigold potion made with water was thought to enable mortals to see fairies if they rubbed it onto their eyelids.

The possession of marigolds was once thought to protect people against the sharp tongues of gossipmongers. For this reason, the flower also became associated with jealousy, although its original meaning was a positive one. In medieval times, marigolds were thought to stave off the plague.

IF YOU LOVE MARIGOLDS, you have an exuberant and cheerful nature. Others are likely to describe you as being like a ray of sunshine. You express gratitude for what you have and count your blessings, which wins you many friends but can also create jealousy.

"Here's flowers for you;
Hot lavender, mints, savory, marjoram;
The marigold, that goes to be bed wi' the sun,
And with him rises weeping; these are flowers
Of middle summer, and I think they are given
To men of middle age."

WILLIAM SHAKESPEARE *THE WINTER'S TALE*, PERDITA IN ACT IV, SCENE IV

Nasturtium

Brought to England in 1574, nasturtiums were first discovered in Mexico and Peru by the conquistadors—hence their meaning of conquest and victory in battle. Nasturtiums might be given as a gift among friends to celebrate the friendship triumphing over time or adversity, or as a way of recognizing a personal or professional victory. Nasturtiums are the fortieth wedding anniversary flower, their meaning appropriate for a relationship that has succeeded in lasting through the ups and downs of life for such a long period of time.

The Quechua Indians of Peru used nasturtium leaves medicinally to treat all kinds of ailments, as they are rich in vitamin C and are a natural antiseptic. The nasturtiums grown by the Quechua Indians had yellow flowers, but today there are different varieties in an array of cheerful reds, yellows, oranges, and creams. The round, lilypad-like leaves with veins radiating out from the center look like fairy umbrellas.

In England, the nasturtium was first known as Indian cress because of the peppery taste of its leaves. Its slightly sharp taste and scent also led to the name nasturtium, which developed from the Latin *nasus tortus*—literally "nose twister" or "convulsed nose." This is a reference to the face people made when sampling the peppery plant, all parts of which are edible. It is this peppery quality that makes the nasturtium symbolic of patriotism. During World War Two, when black pepper was unavailable, people used dried nasturtium seeds as an alternative.

IF YOU LOVE NASTURTIUMS, you have a fighting spirit and great zest for life. You are unshakeable in your loyalty to your friends and discourage malicious gossip of any kind. People feel like they know where they stand with you, which wins you a great deal of respect as well as friendship.

Peony

Once loved by the royal families of China, peonies were used to make floral displays for the imperial palaces. They were known as "the flowers of riches and honor" and the red peony was designated King of the Flowers. Frequently used as a motif in Chinese decoration, peonies became symbolic of good fortune and a happy marriage. Pictured in full bloom, peonies symbolize peace. Their large, showy flowers, produced in spring, are also associated with female beauty and reproduction.

For centuries, peonies have been part of Chinese marriage ceremonies, since they bring good fortune. It is still considered good luck to have vases of cut peony flowers at home, too. Peonies in bloom also signify enduring friendship and were often given as gifts in China.

A Chinese legend relates the story of a peony that was ordered to blossom by Queen Mu. Wanting to exercise her power, Queen Mu ordered all the plants in her city to flower specially at the same time for a party she was giving. They all obeyed her except for the peony and, in her fury, Queen Mu had the plant banished to the countryside. As soon as the peony arrived at its destination among the peasants, it bloomed beautifully. News of this reached Queen Mu and, now even more enraged, she ordered that the peony be burned. Strangely, even after it had been set on fire, the peony carried on blooming. Loved by the common people for its noble spirit and unyielding ways, the peony became symbolic of enduring friendship, loyalty, and honor.

IF YOU LOVE PEONIES, you have high ideals and strongly held values. You are courageous enough to maintain your opinion even when it makes you stand out from the crowd. Since others admire you and find you inspirational—they might even be a little in awe of you—you are likely to achieve great things in life.

Poppy

LOYALTY; FAITH; REMEMBRANCE; CONSOLATION;
SACRIFICE; IMAGINATION; FERTILITY; ETERNAL LIFE;
SLEEP; DREAMS; WEALTH

L ong symbolic of eternal life, poppies were placed in ancient Egyptian burial tombs. The ancient Greeks offered poppies to Demeter, the goddess of fertility, and Diana, goddess of the hunt. Greek athletes were given mixtures of poppy seeds, honey, and wine. The Romans also believed that poppies could help to heal a broken heart.

In a Greek legend, Somnus, the god of sleep, created the poppy to help Ceres, the corn goddess. Ceres searched in vain for her lost daughter, Prosperine, who had been taken to the Underworld by Pluto to be his wife. In her grief, Ceres could not make the corn grow until she was soothed to sleep by poppies and regained enough energy for the corn to sprout again.

In a romantic Chinese legend, the beautiful and courageous Lady Yee was married to Hsiang Yu, a noble warrior, and she accompanied him in all his battles. With defeat imminent, Lady Yee danced with Hsiang Yu's sword in the face of death before killing herself. Poppies sprang up around her grave, symbolic of her loyalty, her honor, and of eternal life.

Due to the opium that can be extracted from some poppy varieties, the flower can symbolize sleep and oblivion. This reference is picked up in the film, *The Wizard of Oz*, when Dorothy falls asleep in a field of poppies.

The red poppy has come to signify sacrifice, and has been a symbol honoring soldiers since the Napoleonic wars. After World War One the fields of Flanders, where so many had died, were covered in red poppies, and their flowers came to symbolize the sacrifice of those who had laid down their lives. White poppies are associated with consolation, the imagination, and dreams, while yellow poppies, also known as Welsh poppies, denote wealth and success.

IF YOU LOVE POPPIES, you believe in the importance of honor and camaraderie in your friendships. You have an extra spiritual dimension to your personality and may well have vivid dreams that provide you with extraordinary insights.

FRIENDSHIP

Sunflower

LOYALTY; CONSTANCY; POWER; RADIANCE; PRIDE;
HAUGHTINESS; ADORATION; HAPPINESS; LONGEVITY

The radiant, sun-like appearance of sunflowers has led to them being a popular subject for artists through the ages, but particularly for the Impressionist and post-Impressionist painters of nineteenth-century France. Their botanical name, *Helianthus*, comes from the Greek word *helios*, meaning "sun," and *anthos*, meaning "flower." In 1532 the Spanish conquistador, Francisco Pizarro, reported seeing the people of the Inca Empire worshipping a giant sunflower as the symbol of the sun, and the priestesses wearing large gold discs in the form of sunflowers. Temples in the Andes mountains have been found decorated with images of sunflowers. In the Americas, people used sunflowers to make oil for food, medicine, and dye. Native Americans even placed bowls of sunflower seeds in the graves of their dead. Other common names for the sunflower include the Marigold of Peru and the Indian Sun.

Most of the meanings attributed to sunflowers come from the way that the flowers turn their heads to follow the sun, signifying loyalty and constancy. For this reason they are the third wedding anniversary flower. Since the Sun gives out dazzling light and heat, sunflowers are also symbolic of power, radiance, and warmth.

Another obvious characteristic of sunflowers is their height and this explains how the meaning of haughtiness was attributed to them. A dwarf sunflower, free of connotations of haughtiness, symbolizes adoration. A Western folklore belief was that if a girl put three such sunflower seeds down her back, she would marry the first boy she met. In China, the primary meaning attached to sunflowers was longevity.

IF YOU LOVE SUNFLOWERS, you are as warm and radiant as the flower itself. You have a powerful presence that, at first, can sometimes make other people feel intimidated. However, with your sunny nature, you are quick to put them at their ease. Your charismatic personality tends to put you naturally in the spotlight.

"Ah! Sunflower, weary of time,
Who countest the steps of the sun;
Seeking after that sweet golden clime
Where the traveller's journey is done."

WILLIAM BLAKE, "AH! SUNFLOWER!"

Sweet pea

Popular during the Victorian era in England, sweet peas became the floral emblem of the subsequent Edwardian period. They featured in displays at nearly every wedding and dinner party, and their dried petals were added to the bowls of pot pourri placed around people's homes. Known as the Queen of Annuals, they derive their Latin name, *Lathyrus odoratus*, from the Greek word *lathyros*, meaning "pea" or "pulse" and the Latin word *odoratus*, meaning "fragrant." John Keats (1795–1821) is believed by some flower historians to have made the first mention of the name sweet pea in his poem "Endymion."

An annual climbing herb that comes originally from Italy, the sweet pea is much loved for 'its fragrant, butterfly-shaped flowers. The plant flowers in the entire spectrum of colors except yellow. According to English folklore, sowing sweet-pea seeds before sunrise on St Patrick's Day (March 17) will result in plants that have larger and more fragrant blossoms. Another superstition is that seeds sown on or after the feasts of St David and St Chad (March 1 and 2 respectively) and before or on the feast of St Benedict (March 21), will bloom best.

In Victorian times, it became the custom to give a bunch of sweet peas after an enjoyable visit to stay with friends. In this way, sweet peas came to be symbolic of happy times spent with friends, and of showing one's appreciation and gratitude for this upon leaving them.

IF SWEET PEAS ARE YOUR FAVORITE FLOWERS, you are motivated by your desire to please others and to make them happy. Your tendency is to neglect your own needs to look after everyone else's. You pay attention to detail, and your personal appearance—as well as that of your home—is likely to be highly decorative. Like the sweet pea itself, you are sweet-natured and pretty to look at.

Zinnia

An annual flowering plant, zinnias bloom exuberantly until the first frost. They have large, showy flowers in a variety of bright colors that symbolize the different emotions of friendship. In many ways, zinnias are the ideal flower to give if you are feeling nostalgic about a friendship and want to re-ignite it or commemorate it.

Zinnias were discovered in the early 1500s in the wilderness of Mexico. However, these zinnias were so dull and unappealing that the Mexican emperor gave them a name meaning "eyesore." Today, a popular common name for the zinnia is garden Cinderella, which signifies the transformation that the flower has gone through.

By developing the zinnia to produce the decorative varieties we know today, botanists produced flowers symbolic of life's journey and the friends we make on the way. Another of the zinnia's common names is "youth and old age," which is a reference to the multiple layers of petals that represent the different stages of life.

Choosing a particular color of zinnia to send to someone enables you to convey a specific message. Scarlet zinnias signify devotion, while white ones symbolize goodness of heart, and yellow zinnias denote the daily remembrance of a loved one. A mixed bouquet of the flowers represents concern and thoughts of absent friends, and remembering fond moments and bygone days of happiness.

IF YOU LOVE ZINNIAS, you are a sociable person who greatly values your friendships. You have a nostalgic side to your personality and probably keep mementos of your past. Friends can rely on you to remember their birthdays and anniversaries, since these traditions are important to you. In turn, your thoughtful and loving nature brings you much appreciation and devotion.

Acknowledgments

I would like to thank Cindy Richards, Dawn Bates, and Sally Powell at CICO Books for their creative expertise; Paul Tilby for design; Ingrid Court-Jones for editing and Sarah Perkins for the illustrations.

About the author

Samantha Gray is the author of a number of books for children and adults, including *The Faerie Book* (CICO Books). She is also a contributor to the Flower Fairy Friends series and has worked on titles ranging from *Magical Moonlight Feast* to *Primrose's Woodland Adventure* and the *Flower Fairy Dress Up Book*. Based in London, she also spends much of her time in County Cork, Ireland, in a house surrounded by enchanted woodland.